ALL YOU WANT TO KNOW ABOUT
Spiritualism
In Day-To-Day Life

R. N. LAKHOTIA

New Dawn

NEW DAWN
a division of Sterling Publishers (P) Ltd.
A-59, Okhla Industrial Area, Phase-II, New Delhi-110020
Tel: 6331238 Fax: 91-11-6331241
E-mail: ghai@nde.vsnl.net.in
www.sterlingpublishers.com

All You Wanted to Know About Spiritualism In Day-To-Day Life
© 2002, R. N. Lakhotia
ISBN 81 207 2477 1

All rights are reserved. No part of this publication may be
reproduced, stored in a retrieval system or transmitted, in any
form or by any means, mechanical, photocopying, recording
or otherwise, without prior written permission of the original
publisher.

Published by Sterling Publishers Pvt. Ltd., New Delhi-110020.
Lasertypeset by Vikas Compographics, New Delhi-110020.
Printed at : Shagun Offset Press, New Delhi-29

Contents

About the author	5
1. Integrated Living is Possible Through Spirituality	7
2. Self-Realisation and Living With God	24
3. How to Maximise Happiness and Spiritual Joy	51
4. Experiencing Truth, Beauty and Love in Daily Life	67
5. Food Habits for Ethics and Better Health	77
6. Tackling Adverse Situations and Tragedies	91
7. Right Approach Towards *Karma* or Work in Daily Life	105
8. Purity of Mind, Heart and Action in Daily Life	113
9. Positive Attitude to Avoid Stress and Tension	127
10. Selfless Service to All Creatures	144

About the author

R. N. Lakhotia
R. N. Lakhotia is a well-known authority on taxation in the country. He is a regular writer and the editor of several books on income-tax, vegetarianism, better living and humour and a regular column, "Tax-Doctor", for the *Times of India*. His books have seen over 400 editions. He is the founder President of Income-tax Payers' Association and Rajasthani Academy and a life trustee of the Hindi Bhawan. He is active in social and cultural activities

and was District Governor of Lions' Club International. He is the Principal of Lakhotia College of Taxation and Management; he is also life patron and president of Indian Vegetarian Congress, Northern India, and has strongly taken up the cause of vegetarianism.

The author stays at:
"Lakhotia Niwas"
S-228, Greater Kailash-II
New Delhi-110048
Tel: 6415434

Integrated Living is Possible through Spirituality

Living with a spiritual purpose

We live either a happy meaningful life or a miserable one. The choice depends on us. Either we can have materialism as the main aim of our life or we can choose both material progress and spiritual principles in day-to-day life. Fortunately, the latter is possible. It was the Nobel Prize winner, Albert Schweitzer, who in his books *Out of My Life and Thought* (p. 126) opined, "Affirmation of life is the spiritual act by which a man ceases to live unreflectively and begins to devote himself to his life with a reverence in order to raise it through its true value. To affirm life is to deepen, to make more inward, and to exalt the will-to-live".

Thus, it is possible to live well and make living worthwhile. The purpose of our living should be to have spiritual bliss in day-to-day life. Our happiness has to blossom in the social and spiritual space because our human nature is such that we cannot be truly happy by being self-centred.

Therefore, the purpose of our living should be to lead a spiritual life, namely, with God on one side and with those around us, on the other. To live a spiritual life, is to live life in all its fullness. This requires the integration of the three dimensions of human life, namely, the physical, mental and spiritual. Most human beings tend to live only in terms of one of these three components, mostly the physical. This is the case especially in the materialistic and consumeristic culture of the present time. In such an environment, to be able to lead a full life, we should remember that a human being is not only a body but also a mind and a soul at once. And spirituality involves the dynamic integration of all the three dimensions. Therefore, the purpose of living should be to achieve this dynamic integration to live life fully.

The Vedantic way of life

There are various religions and sects in the world and each religion professes to have some spiritual principles for day-to-day life but the *Vedanta*, as Swami Vivekananda said (CW5 : 306), "is the essence of all religions." Thus, the *Vedanta* is not a new religion but is as old as God

Himself. It is not confined to any time and place, it is everywhere. Hence, the principles of the *Vedanta* which are given in a capsule form in the *Bhagavad Gita* form the basis of spiritualism in day-to-day life as discussed in this book. The *Bhagavad Gita* is the most popular scripture of India which contains the essence of spiritualism in everyday life. It is the revelation of the higher self to the lower self. In the spiritual struggle that rises constantly in our hearts, we are like Arjuna, trembling with fear, blinded by delusion, not knowing what to do. It is His voice that can put courage and breathe a new life into us, and make us rise and walk. The *Gita* is the breath of this new life. It is the nectar which can make us invincible and immortal. Aldous Huxley described it as one of the clearest and most comprehensive summaries of perennial philosophy ever to have been made. As Adi Shankaracharya puts it, the *Gita* is the quintessence of wisdom. Guidance for exalted living in day-to-day life is found in the various *shlokas* or verses of the *Gita*. Some of the most important of these verses, which will help us in achieving spiritualism in our day-to-day lives, are quoted in this book.

The *Vedanta* also means the culmination, or the deepest mysteries of the *Vedas*. It is a way of life and an exhortation to realise the ultimate truth which can be attained through long practice. The Supreme Spirit is often referred to in the *Vedanta* as *Sat-Cit-Ananda*, that is, being, intelligence and bliss. The *Vedanta* points out that God is the only reality, all creation or separate existence is *maya* or illusion. The *Upanisads* together with the *Bhagavad Gita* and Badarayana's *Brahmasutras* constitute the doctrine of the *Vedanta*. The Supreme Spirit of which we are a part is also referred to as *Brahman*. It helps us in overcoming the fear of death. The *Vedanta* helps us to know our real being which puts an end to our suffering. In the words of Paramahansa Yogananda, "The joy of God-realization is boundless, unceasing, all the time new. Body or mind — nothing can disturb you when you are in that consciousness - such is the grace and glory of the Lord." Thus, the *Vedanta* is all-comprehensive. It includes every stage, every process of spiritual practice and is the true guide for our everyday life.

Integration of virtues

The *Vedanta* is specific, as well as universal. It not only has its all embracing, universal aspect but also its specific aspect, which originated in India and is the distilled wisdom of the Hindu spiritual tradition. The hallmark of both the dimensions would be an integrated life, which moves smoothly, resolutely and joyfully towards the goal of spiritual awakening. This integrated life is the real reason why we engage in a particular activity and sometimes it is also the reason why we do not engage in some other activity. And our life activities, both private and public, reflect our most cherished and deeply-held beliefs about the ultimate reality and our relationship to it. This also includes our relationship with all other beings on the planet.

The ultimate aim of all life activities is the attainment of a spiritual life. In attempting to live a spiritual life, we are attaining what is our birth right as human beings. This is because we human beings are free neither in the material nor in the mental realm. We are free only in the sphere of the spirit. The spirit is pure freedom which leads us unto truth and sets us free.

In fact, no human being or society can be truly free unless its freedom is established firmly on its spiritual foundation. Conversely, spiritual life is marked by creative freedom - the freedom to love, to create, to care and to share through the integration of these great virtues in the true spirit. When we march towards a spiritual life, we find that the darkness of hatred, cruelty and exploitation is negated. The vedic prayer, "Lead us from darkness to light, from untruth to truth, from death to eternal life", contains the essence of our spiritual life.

Educational curriculum on spirituality

To enable students to have their foundations in spirituality right from the beginning, suggestions have been made from time to time to include ethical values and spirituality in the educational curriculum of the students. In this context, it is worth mentioning the proposal of the National Council of Educational Research and Training to introduce a new curriculum for secondary education with emphasis on spiritual development. The initiative would certainly be laudatory if it inculcates in our children such universal values like love, charity and forgiveness and promotes inter-faith harmony and respect for all religions. When we keep our hearts and minds open, we can encounter God, even amid the cacophonous chaos of our daily lives. The best representatives of the infinite love of God are our parents. In a mother's selflessness and compassion, we can envisage the unconditional nature of divine love. Similarly, in a father's guidance and endeavour to provide for his child, we get a glimpse of the eternal care and peace that the heavenly Father promises us in His world. Similarly, in a child's innocence, we can see another facet of God, namely forgiveness. Students should be taught that God is manifest in all forms. Hence, a reverent attitude towards the entire creation is the most powerful way to seek God. This is what comprises spiritualism in day-to-day life.

Live every day
The best way of ensuring spirituality in day-to-day life is to live every day fully and well. We should be content to be alive from morning until bedtime. We should live peacefully, patiently, lovingly and purely till the sun goes down. And this is all that

life really means. The answer to the question 'What is life?' is very difficult as well as very easy. Schodinger was not the first to ask the question 'What is life?' nor will he be the last. In fact, life is a mysterious energy and the answer to the question is illusive. If we cultivate the habit of living every moment of our lives fully, we are able to live life well. We should not be unduly upset by the happenings of the past and bother ourselves with unnecessary anxieties and worries of the future. This way, we can enjoy what is known as blissful living. In this connection, Emerson has very rightly said, "Finish every day and be done with it. You have done what you could; some blunders and absurdities crept in; forget them as soon as you can. Tomorrow is a new day; you shall take it well and serenely and with too high a spirit not to be encumbered with your own nonsense."

To conclude, here is a poem that Sir William Osler always kept on his desk. This poem was written by the Indian dramatist, Kalidas:

"Salutation to the dawn
Look to this day!

For it is life, the very life of life.
In its brief course, lie all the verities and realities of your existence;
> *The bliss of growth*
> *The glory of action*
> *The splendour of beauty.*

For yesterday is but a dream and tomorrow is only a vision, but today, well-lived makes every yesterday a dream of happiness
And every tomorrow a vision of hope.
Look well, therefore, to this day;
Such is the salutation to the dawn."

Self-Realisation and Living with God

Self-realisation is possible in this life

Self-realisation or self-knowledge or God-realisation is the goal of human life. It is ignorance which is the root cause of all ills and which gives rise to the ego and obscures the world of non-dual reality. What is desirable, therefore, is to worship everything as God—every form as his temple. Only then can we have spirituality in day-to-day living.

We should remember that the self or the spirit or the *atman* is essentially ever pure, ever luminous and ever free. It is different from the body or mind complex. When we go into the genetic system or the body, and are controlled by it, the light of the *atman* does not shine clearly. Hence, we have to make it shine truly in its own form. This is known as self-realisation. Great sages, not only in India but in other parts of the world, throughout the ages, have done it. It is the first right of all human beings. And it can be done by getting our minds purified and released from the control of our selves and realising our own infinite dimensions. Lord Krishna in the *Bhagavad Gita* (IV. 10) has uttered this truth as:

"*Vitaragabhayakrodha*
   manmaya mam upasritah
bahavo jnanatapasa
   puta madbhavam agatah"

This has been translated by Dr. S. Radhakrishnan as:

"Delivered from passion, fear and anger, absorbed in Me, taking refuge in Me, many purified by the austerity of wisdom, have attained to My state of being."

It is only when we realise that there is a vast spiritual treasure within us, and when we become restless to realise it, do we awaken to that light. What we have to remember is that the goal of human life is liberation while living. And this liberation is the attainment of equilibrium of consciousness; it can be realised even in this world, for *Brahman* is in everything and everywhere.

When we constantly endeavour to focus our mind on self-realisation, we are able to think of self or God at the time of death and this ensures liberation from life. This is confirmed by Lord Krishna in the *Bhagavad Gita* (VIII.5):

"Antakale ca man eva
  smaran muktva kalevaram
yah prayati sa madbhavam
  yati nasty atra samsayah"

This has been translated by Dr. S. Radhakrishnan as:

"And whoever, at the time of death, gives up his body and departs, thinking of Me alone, he comes to My status (of being): of that there is no doubt."

God should be the central theme of our life

Liberation from the cycle of births and deaths is possible only through self-realisation which also leads to the contemplation of God. The central theme of living should be remembering God and seeing Him in other creatures as our own *atman* or self.

What is God? He is not different from our own self. This is why the great saint Swami Vivekananda says that human beings are essentially divine and we have to manifest the divinity in us. This aspect of God as our own self is very beautifully described by Lord Krishna in the *Bhagavad Gita* (X.20) as:

*"Aham atma gudakesa
 sarvabhutasayasthitah*

> *aham adis ca madhyam ca*
> *bhutanam anta eva ca"*

This is translated by Dr. S. Radhakrishnan as:

"I, O Gudakes (Arjuna), am the self seated in the hearts of all creatures. I am the beginning, the middle and the very end of beings."

Spirituality centring on God is important in almost all walks of life. Vedic teachings point to the conclusion that the inner self is verily *Brahman* or God and He is without parallel.

The *Kathopanishaa* has solved the mystery of the hidden God in these immortal words, "Just as fire is hidden in wood and butter in milk, God dwells within everything in the cosmos, but due to ignorance we are unaware of His divine presence."

God can be worshipped in different ways

Ramakrishna Paramhansa had a very important saying about the worship of God. His favourite words were: "*Joto Mat Toto Path*". He used to say, "In a potter-shop there are vessels of different shapes and forms - pots, jars, dishes, plates, etc. but all are made of the same clay. So God is one, but he is worshipped in different ages and climes under different names and aspects." Ultimately all paths lead to the same goal i.e., God-realisation. The only requirement is that our devotion to God should be very sincere and firm. This is confirmed by Lord Krishna in the *Gita* (IV.11):

"Ye yatha mam prapadyante
 tams tathai'va bhajamy aham
 mama vartmanuvartante
 manusyah partha sarvasah"

This has been translated by Dr. S. Radhakrishnan in his world famous commentary on the *Bhagavad Gita* as under:

"As men approach me so do I accept them: men on all sides follow my path, O Partha (Arjuna)." This resolves all disputes about the different ways of God worship.

Yoga in daily life

Yoga - whether *Bhakti yoga* or *Karma yoga* or *Jnana yoga* or any other type of *yoga*, should be an integral part of life for practising spirituality in daily life. The *Bhagavad Gita* combines *Karma yoga*, which advocates selfless and dedicated service, *Bhakti yoga*, which inculcates the spirit of total surrender to the Almighty, and *Jnana yoga*, which teaches that the self within us is nothing but the supreme, all-pervading self. The main reason behind the formulation of three different paths, based on the three different faculties, to achieve a single goal of human attainment is that the minds of all men are not alike. In each individual, any one of the three faculties is more dominant than the others.

Karma yoga about which the *Gita* speaks is the path of spiritual attainment through desireless action performed with an attitude that work is worship. *Karma yoga* is not contrary to *Jnana yoga*. A *Karma yogi* also reaches through selfless action the same state of knowledge or wisdom as that of a *Jnana yogi*. When we have staunch and unflinching faith in oneness with God and regard Him as our own, then God in return will also consider us as His own.

Whoever feels God's presence in everybody will not cause harm or injury to anybody. Rabiya was a great lady and a saint of Arabia. Once a saint came to her house and asked Rabiya to come out of the house and see the beauty and manifestation of

God in nature. Rabiya did not come out and replied from inside the house: "You may see the beauty of the creation of God from outside. I have *darshan* or glimpse of the shadow of God in the depth of my heart."

One may also follow *Jnana yoga* which is the path of knowledge towards experiencing the ultimate. Self-purification is the first step for *Jnana yoga*. When the light comes, darkness goes. So also, when knowledge dawns, ignorance vanishes. Therefore, *jnana* is not only the goal but it is also the path to achieve that goal.

Another *yoga* which is akin to *Jnana yoga* is *Raja yoga*, a particular form of *yoga* propounded by the great Rishi Patanjali.

Yoga means union. The human being who seeks union with God is called a *yogi*. The detached worker is called a *Karma yogi*. He who seeks the union through love is called a *Bhakti yogi*. He who seeks it through mysticism is called a *Raja yogi*. And, he who seeks it through philosophy is called the *Jnana yogi*. Each one of them tells us to cling to our reason and to hold fast to it. What is essential, as Swami Vivekananda says is that all these *yogas*, in one form or the other, should actually be carried out in practice. Religion is realisation and not mere talk or doctrine. It is being and becoming, and not hearing or acknowledging. It is the whole soul changing into what it believes. This is practical spirituality.

Patanjali's eight-fold path of *yoga*
The great Rishi Patanjali in his famous *Yogasutras* (II.29), has given the eight limbs of *yoga* as under:

1. *Yama*, i.e., abstention from evil doing,

2. *Niyama*, i.e., the various observances,
3. *Asana*, i.e., posture,
4. *Pranayama*, i.e., control of the *prana*,
5. *Pratyahara*, i.e., withdrawal of the mind from sense objects,
6. *Dharna*, i.e., concentration,
7. *Dhyana*, i.e., meditation, and
8. *Samadhi*, i.e., absorption in the *atman*.

The five *yamas* refer to abstention from others, from falsehood, from theft, from incontinence and from greed. These forms of abstenion are basic rules of conduct. They must be practised every day without any reservation as to time, place, purpose or caste rules. The five *niyamas* or observances are purity, contentment, mortification, study of scriptures and devotion to God. About *ahimsa* or non-violence in daily life, Patanjali says that when a human being becomes steadfast in his abstention from harming others, then all living creatures will cease to feel enmity in his presence. Likewise, when a person becomes steadfast in his abstention from falsehood, he gets the power of obtaining for himself and for others, the fruits of good deeds without having to perform the deeds themselves. When a person becomes steadfast in his abstention from theft, all wealth comes to him. When a person becomes steadfast in his abstention from incontinence, he acquires spiritual energy. When a man becomes steadfast in his abstention from greed, he gains knowledge of his past, present and future existences. By observing these *yamas* and *niyamas*, Patanjali maintains that one achieves purification of the heart, cheerfulness of mind, power of concentration, control of the passions and fitness for vision of the *atman*. By practising the various observances or *niyamas*, one gains supreme happiness. As a result of mortification or self-discipline, impurities are removed. Then special powers come to the body and the sense organs. As a result of the study of scriptures, one obtains the vision of that aspect of God which one has chosen to worship. As a result of devotion to God, one achieves *samadhi*.

The other six limbs of *yoga* as per Patanjali are also not difficult to be practised in daily life. The third limb of *yoga* is *asana* or posture: it means to be seated in a position which is firm but relaxed. Posture becomes firm and relaxed through control of the natural tendencies of the body, and through meditation on the infinite. After mastering the postures, one must practise control of the *prana* (*pranayama*) by regulating the motions of inhalation and exhalation. The mind gets purified through the practice of *pranayama*, ignorance is gradually dispensed and the light of spiritual discrimination between the real and the unreal is seen. When the mind is withdrawn from the sense objects, the sense objects also withdraw themselves from their respective objects and thus are said to imitate the mind. This is known as the fifth limb of *yoga*, or *pratyahara*. The sixth limb of *yoga* is *dharna* or concentration, which means the mind is at the centre of the spiritual consciousness in the body; it is fixed on some divine form, either within the body or outside it. Then comes the seventh limb of *yoga*, namely *dhyana* or meditation which means an unbroken flow of thought towards the object of concentration.

When, in meditation, the true nature of the object shines forth, that is, when the self shines and is not distorted by the mind of the perceived, the condition is called absorption or *samadhi*.

When these three - concentration, meditation and absorption - are brought to bear upon one subject, they are called *samyama*. Rishi Patanjali says that through mastery of *samyama* comes the light of knowledge and it has to be practised in day-to-day life.

Meditation for God-realisation

As mentioned above, one very important limb of Patanjali's eight-fold path of *yoga* is *dhyana* or meditation, which ultimately helps us in God-realisation. In one sense, it means intense, concentrated thinking. The *Gita* also emphasises the importance of meditation. It does not consider right action alone to be enough for right living. Right living can be all compreshensive only when *dhyana yoga* or meditation is made an integral part of it. Lord Krishna in the *Gita* (IX.22) has declared:

"Ananyas cintayanto mam
  ye janah paryupasate
kesam nityabhiyuktanam
  yogaksemam vahamyaham"

This is translated by Dr. S. Radhakrishnan as:

"But those who worship Me, meditating on Me alone, to them who ever persevere, I bring attainment of what they have not and security in what they have."

It should be practised on the *atman* or the self. Though the task is very hard, by practise (*abhyasa*) and dispassion (*vairagya*), it is possible to bring it to concentrate on the *atman* or the self. Meditation should, as far as possible, be at the same time and preferably in the early hours of the morning to reap best results towards self-realisation.

Surrender to God
In our life, we might come across situations when conflicting views or opinions or thoughts on God or God-realisation are presented before us. In such cases, the only way of God-

realisation is complete surrender and faith in God to help us attain true knowledge. Lord Krishna has proclaimed in the *Gita* (XVIII.66):

"Sarvadharmam parityajya
 mamekam saranam vraja
aham tvam sarvapapebhyo
 moksayisyami ma sucah"

This has been translated by Dr. S. Radhakrishnan as under:

"Abandoning all duties, come to Me alone for shelter. Be not grieved, for I shall release thee from all evils."

We should willingly yield to His pressure, completely surrender to His will and take shelter in His love. Thus, if we replace self-confidence by perfect confidence in God, it is sure that He will save us. God asks of us total self-giving and gives us in return the power of the spirit which changes every situation.

Arjuna was perturbed by the various duties, ritualistic and ethical, and the fact that the war will result in the confusion of castes and indifference to ancestors, besides violation of the sacred duty of reverence for teachers. Krishna told him not to worry about these laws and usages but to trust Him and bow to Him. He told Arjuna that if he consecrated his life, actions, feelings and thoughts, and surrendered himself to God, He would guide him through the fight of life so that he need not have any fear. Therefore, surrender is the easiest way to self-transcendence or self-realisation.

How to Maximise Happiness and Spiritual Joy

Everyone longs for happiness. We should remember that the need of our real nature is *anand* or happiness; this is because the human being has in him the divine spark of *Brahman* or God who is also called *Sachidananda*. We are essentially happy beings. It is only because of our negative thoughts of pessimism, jealousy and anger that we become unhappy. Therefore, we should dispel all negative thoughts by constant practise. We should remember what Swami Muktananda has said in this connection: "Reform yourself more and more every day; think higher and nobler thoughts." Tolstoy's advice is also worth remembering, "If you want to be happy, be." Emerson has rightly said, "Happiness is a perfume you cannot pour on others without getting a few drops on yourself." We would also do well to remember the advice of William Henry Channing in this context: "To live content with small means, to seek elegance rather than luxury, and refinement rather than fashion; to be worthy, not respectable and wealthy, not rich, to study hard, think quietly, talk gently, act frankly; to listen to the stars and birds, to babes and sages, with open heart; to bear on cheerfully, do all bravely awaiting occasions, worry never; in a word, to like the spiritual, unbidden and unconscious, grow up through the common."

In this chapter, we have discussed some of the positive things which we should do to have happiness in our everyday life.

1. Control of mind

Happiness is a mental state and not merely a physical one. Hence, control of mind becomes very important for remaining happy in day-to-day life. To have complete control over the mind we should strengthen our will power. One who has no control over the mind cannot have peace of mind. And one who has no peace of mind cannot have happiness. Through control of mind we can achieve spiritual illumination. This is because a controlled mind can easily concentrate. We should, however, remember that those who have no moral principles guiding their life and have no regularity in life cannot control their minds. Hence, we have to bring discipline to our lives. Meditating on God is the most effective way of doing this.

2. Cultivate the magic quality of love

A fundamental value to be cultivated and practised in day-to-day life is love, which is the manifestation of the divine in the human heart. Love is the source of all life. It is the hunger of the human soul for divine beauty. It is love which resolves all conflicts between man and man. It is the divine spark revolving in the mind, feeling and will, all things that are strong, deep and enduring. In short, love is such a virtue which results in uninterrupted happiness in us as well as in the people around us. Love is the soil in which the loved one grows, it enriches him without limiting or restricting him. We should love our friends, relatives, neighbours and the persons with whom we come into contact and this love should be a selfless love. It is only through selfless love that we get maximum happiness. As Coleridge said:

> "He prayeth best who loveth best,
> all things both great and small,
> For the dear God who loveth us,
> made and loveth all."

We should remember that in love alone — love of God and love of human beings — we shall find the solution of all the ills which afflict the world today.

3. Why envy?

We should remember that a great enemy of happiness is envy. Josh Billings rightly said about envy, "Show me what a man envies the life in others and I will show you what he has got most of himself." Envy may not do any harm to others but it certainly burns the elements of happiness in our hearts and causes unnecessary bitterness and destroys happiness.

4. Forgive others

One of the greatest factors which contributes to happiness is the quality of forgiveness. Once we forgive the other person, the seeds of bitterness in our heart are also removed, thereby paving the way for happiness. Remember what George Herbert said about forgiveness: "He who cannot forgive others breaks the bridge over which he must pass himself; for every man has a need to be forgiven."

5. Forgive yourself too

We should not only forgive the other person but also forgive ourselves and not indulge in remembering and repenting on our past mistakes. We should rather take a lesson from our past mistakes and resolve not to commit the same in future. We should develop self-love and not self-contempt. If we cannot love ourselves, we cannot love others also. We should remember that we owe a duty to ourselves. The Bible says: "Thou shalt love thy neighbours as thyself." Medical science has proved that lack of self-love is at the root of many mental illnesses. Dr. Robert H. Felix, former Director of the National Institute of Mental Health in Washington, USA, says a person has self-love when, "one has a feeling of dignity, of worthwhileness, a feeling of adequacy - yet a healthy sense of humility."

6. Have a cheerful disposition and a smile

Another element of happiness is a cheerful disposition. We should cultivate the habit of wearing a smile on our face at all times. We should remember that a smile costs nothing but creates much. It enriches those who receive it without impoverishing those who give. We should remember to be cheerful by remembering what Saint Francis said, "It is not seemingly that a servant of God should show a sad and troubled face before his brethren." We would do well to remember what the Mother of Pondicherry said: "Learn to smile always and in all circumstances; to smile at your sorrows as well as your joys, your sufferings as well as your hopes, for in a smile there is a sovereign power of self-mastery."

7. Don't be a grievance collector

We should always cultivate the habit of remaining calm and cool and not being angry at everything. We should remember not to unload bitterness and resentment on innocent friends and neighbours. We come across occasions which might arouse a genuine cause for grievance. But we must not suffer from a grievance-collecting fever. We should not allow a grievance to sink unresolved into our sub-conscious mind and to breed like a poisonous bacteria in our emotional bloodstream. Even if there is a genuine grievance we should not put it in a glass case and then gloat over the same. Rather, we should travel with a lighter heart and be a happier person in everyday life.

8. Remember the distinction between acceptance and expectation

A good deal of happiness is lost when there are unhappy moments in our day-to-day life. Fortunately, most of such moments can be avoided. Most of the time, we tend to be angry with the members of our family or close friends when they do not come up to our expectations. Happiness is the result of acceptance of facts and the effect of not having too many expectations from our family and friends.

9. Recognise your dual nature - selfishness and selflessness

A human being has a dual nature. If he is selfish, he is selfless too. We often experience joy when we give; this is because when we give, we basically satisfy the inner desire to give of ourselves for the betterment of the less fortunate. This is the cheapest and most effective mental therapy available today. For our own happiness and spiritual joy we should do selfless service quietly and without any thought of reward by remembering the beautiful words of William Wordsworth when he spoke of : "That portion of a good man: his little nameless, unremembered acts of kindness and of love."

10. Spiritual joy

Real spiritual joy comes through being optimistic and having full faith in God. We have discussed elsewhere the value of full faith in God for excellent living. Lack of faith in God paralyses the hope and confidence of mankind. We should remember the happy moments of our life. Meditation and surrender to God, as explained elsewhere, will enable us to continously have spiritual joy and bliss.

Experiencing Truth, Beauty and Love in Daily Life

Truth is the corner-stone of spiritual living

One of the greatest qualities necessary for spiritual living is truth. The *Rig Veda* proclaims loudly, "*Ekam sad vipra bahuda vadanti*", i.e., "Truth is one, the sages describe it variously." The *Brihadaranayaka Upanishad* contains an important message for spiritual living, "There is nothing higher than *dharma*. Verily, that which is *dharma*, is truth." The

Mundakopanishad says, "Truth always triumphs, not falsehood. It is by truth that the path of the sages becomes free from obstacles. The path of the sages whose worldly desires have been satisfied or overcome is the one that leads to God, the Supreme Soul." Thus, we find that God is truth and truth is God. Truth is fact, falsehood fiction; truth is existence, falsehood illusion; truth is reality, falsehood superstition. Man's destiny is to search for truth. Maharshi Dayanand has rightly said, "A truthful person is not afraid of death." But our scriptures say that we should not just speak the truth, but speak it in such a manner that it does not hurt others. This very thought has been conveyed by Henry David Thoreau who said, "The only way to speak the truth is to speak lovingly."

Swami Vivekananda (CWI.189) once said, "Through truth everything is attained." That is why his guru Ramkrishna Paramhansa could renounce everything except truth. Thus, truth is both the way and the goal, direction to the destination and the destination itself. Our object in living a spiritual life should be to become a true person. A true person is one who is wholly detached and utterly free. Hence, truth is the corner-stone of spiritual life.

Beauty is an essential aspect of spiritual living

Albert Einstein once said, "The ideals which have lighted my way, and time after time have given me new courage to face life cheerfully, have been kindness, beauty and truth... The trite subjects of human efforts — possessions, outward success, luxury — have always seemed to me contemptible." John Keats's immortal lines on truth and beauty are well-known: "Beauty is truth, truth beauty, That is all ye know on earth, and all ye need to know." An attractive personality is like a beautiful garden. It is important to plant the right seeds—the seeds of love—and to tend them carefully so that they grow in strength and beauty.

Anything which is not beautiful is worth discarding. This is what William Morris in *The Beauty of Life* (1880), said, "If you want a golden rule that will fit everybody, this is it: have nothing in your houses that you do not know to be useful, or believe to be beautiful."

Love is an important ingredient for spiritual living

Love is an important element of happiness. It has been described differently on different occasions. Swami Chidbhavananda said, "Love permeates the universe. Love manifests itself as lust at the physical level. As sex attraction, it engenders jealousy, poisons the system and clouds the mind. Pure love is constructive. It ever gives, never seeks. It is free from fear. He who practises pure love evolves in divinity. Love makes life charming. It overcomes obstacles. It sanctifies the family. It unites the world. It beautifies the ugly. It converts hell into heaven. Let the mind be imbued with love." Swami Jyotirmayananda described the different types of love in the following words:

"Though love in its intrinsic form is of the very nature of the divine self, it expresses through various forms in human life. Love for inferiors is called *anugraha* (gracious love). Love for equals is called *prem* (love in general parlance). Love for elders is termed *shraddha* (love blended with faith and reverence). Love for one's beloved is *pranaya* (melting love). Love for God is called *bhakti* (devotion)."

The great Russian writer, Fyodor Dostoevski says: "Love all God's creation, both the whole and every grain of sand. Love every leaf, every ray of light. Love the animals, love the plants, love each separate thing. If thou love each thing thou will perceive the mystery of God in all; and when once thou perceive this, thou wilt thenceforward grow every day to a fuller understanding of it; until thou come at last to love the whole world with a love that will then be all-embracing and universal."

Swami Vivekananda's views on love inspire us to have love in daily life: "All expansion is life, all contraction is death. All love is expansion, all selfishness is contraction. Love is, therefore, the only law of life. He who loves, lives, he who is selfish is dying. Therefore, love for love's sake because it is the only law of life, just as you breathe to live."

Similar is the view of Swami Shivananda: "Love is a mysterious divine glue that unites the hearts of all. It is a divine magical healing balm of very high potency. A life without faith, love and devotion is a dreary waste. Love is divine. Love is the greatest power on earth. It is irresistible. It is love alone that can really conquer the heart of a man. Love subdues the enemy. Love can tame wild animals. Its power is infinite. Its depth is unfathomable. Its nature is ineffable. Its glory is indescribable."

Conclusion

I remember that once a respectable old lady was asked, "What gives you such a lovely complexion? Which cosmetic do you use?" The lady replied sweetly, "I use for the lips, truth; for the voice, prayer; for the hands, charity; for the figure, uprightness; and for the heart, love."

Food Habits for Ethics and Better Health

Moderation in food habits for good living

Our thoughts and actions in life are moulded by the type of food we eat. The food can be *satvik* or *rajasik* or *tamasik*. *Satvik* food is the best of all. (See *Gita*: XVII.8)

"*Ayuhsattvabalarogya
    sukhapritivivardhanah
rasyah snigdhah sthira hrydya
    aharah satvikpriyah*"

This means that the food which augments life, energy, strength, health, happiness and joy, which is savoury, delicious, nourishing and agreeable, is liked by the *satvik*. Hence, our aim in life should be to eat *satvik* food as far as possible. And, most of the vegetarian food, particularly fruits and vegetables, etc., is *satvik*. No non-vegetarian food can ever be *satvik*. Hence, for spiritual living, we should only eat *satvik* or *rajasik* vegetarian food. We should be moderate in food habits, as per the advice of Lord Krishna in the *Gita* (VI.17), where it is said that:

"*Yuktaharaviharasya*
 yuktacestasya karmasu

yuktasvapnavabodhasya
  yogo bhavati dukhhaha."

The above verse means: He who is moderate in food and movements, in his engagement, in action and in sleep and wakefulness, attains to *yoga* which destroys misery.

Why should I remain a vegetarian?

There is a growing acceptance in the West that vegetarianism is more modern and scientific and a better way of living than flesh-eating. Medical authorities throughout the world have agreed that the vegetarian diet is ideal for promoting good health. For example, fruits, vegetables, pulses, nuts and milk products provide a balanced diet which does not turn into toxins in our system. An animal killed becomes dead matter but this is not so with vegetables. It has also been proved by the researchers that at the time of killing an animal, it gets frightened and toxic elements enter its body. From there, they enter the body of the person who eats meat and this adversely affects his health. Leading medical authorities like Dr. Michael Klaper, Dr. M.S. Brown and Dr. J. L. Goldstein have proved that non-vegetarian food, including eggs, lack vitamin B-Complex, vitamin C, calcium and carbohydrate. Nature has intended human beings to be vegetarians. If we compare the physical nature of the flesh-eating animals, we find that they have long teeth to tear the raw animal flesh. Cows, monkeys, horses and other vegetarian animals have flat teeth for grinding vegetarian foods. Meat-eating animals have rough tongues to lick flesh from the bone. The intestines of meat-eating animals are about two to three times their body's length so that the meat which they eat can pass through their system clearly before it purifies. But the intestines of the herbivorous animals are about six to seven times their body's length. Human beings have flat grinding teeth like the vegetarian animals. Our intestines are also about six to seven times our body's length like the vegetarian animals'. Hence, we can say that God has made human beings to be vegetarians only.

For ethical reasons also, many of the greatest men of the world, like Aristotle, Plato, Socrates, Leonardo da Vinci, Shakespeare, Dr. Huxley, Einstein, George Bernard Shaw, H.G. Wells, Annie Besant, Leo Tolstoy, Shelley, Rousseau and

Emerson have been vegetarians. When we cannot give life to any animal, we have no right to take their life too. Further, the more developed the expression of consciousness in a particular form of life, the more pain it feels when we destroy it. For all these reasons, and particularly for reasons of health as explained below, it is very important to remain a vegetarian all our life in our own interest. This would ensure healthy living and greater spiritual progress.

Nutritional aspects of vegetarian food

Vegetarian food has all the necessary elements required for good health as compared to non-vegetarian diet, as is seen from the chart given below where a comparison is made between the nutrition value of 100 gms. of vegetarian food as compared to the same amount of non-vegetarian food. The source is the Health Bulletin No. 23, Government of India:

(per 100 gms.)

Name of food stuff	Protein	Minerals	Carbohydrates	Calories
Vegetarian food				
Green Gram	24.0	3.6	56.6	334
Soyabeans	43.2	4.6	20.9	432
Groundnut	31.9	2.3	19.3	549
Skimmed milk powder	38.3	6.8	51.0	357
Non-vegetarian foods				
Egg	13.3	1.9	Nil	173
Fish	22.6	0.8	Nil	91
Mutton	18.5	1.3	Nil	194

Give due importance to eating fruits and vegetables

As far as possible, we should eat fruits only in the morning, for breakfast. We can have regular food consisting of cereals, pulses and vegetables at lunch and dinner time but, as far as possible, cereals and snacks should be avoided at breakfast time. We should not eat anything between meals. We may take fresh juices. We should avoid cola and alcoholic drinks and liquor.

Spirituality helps in curing arthritis
One of the common ailments which is on the increase these days throughout the world is arthritis. People who use religion and spirituality to cope with the chronic pain of rheumotoid arthritis, reduce their pain and boost their sense of well-being, as per the report by Keith

Mulvihill in the *Times of India*, New Delhi edition of April 19, 2001. Dr. Francis J. Keefe of Duke University Medical School in Durham, North Carolina, and his colleagues have written, "One might expect that people coping with chronic illness or chronic pain might find it difficult to maintain a positive outlook or feel connected to God or the beauty of life. The results of this study suggest otherwise. Persons who reported of being able to control and decrease pain using positive religious and spiritual strategies to cope with them were less likely to experience joint pains and more likely to experience positive mood and higher levels of social support." These authors stress that these spiritual experiences were not unusual phenomena, but rather those that ordinary people have in the context of daily life.

Compassion and good living go together

The essence of vegetarianism is *ahimsa* or non-violence, that is, the spirit of compassion towards all living creatures. In the *Mahabharata* 69/37-43, Damayanti says to Nala, "Compassion is the highest virtue." It is universally believed that for the practice of ethical values, we should give the same treatment to others as we expect from them. However, this ethical virtue can be practised in the true spirit only when we have the quality of compassion in us. In *Tirukkural*, which is considered as the fifth Tamil *Veda* and is written by the great Tamil saint Thiruvalluvar, it is said:

"The best of all possessions is the wealth of compassion

For the meanest of men too possess worldly wealth."

Compassion is a great quality which helped Abraham Lincoln, the world famous President of USA, achieve greatness. Once in the New Orleans town of USA, Abraham Lincoln was greatly moved by the sight of a Negro being tied to a post and beaten mercilessly. The spirit of compassion arose to such an extent that Lincoln decided to abolish slavery and achieved a historical feat. It is this quality of compassion which made various eminent personalities of the world turn vegetarian, as mentioned earlier. Hence, for spiritual living we must practise the quality of compassion in our everyday life.

Tackling Adverse Situations and Tragedies

Tragic situations are normal

In our day-to-day life we often come across tragic situations and adverse circumstances. The art of right living lies in coping with adverse situations, tragedies and bereavements. Who has not encountered a tragedy in his life? Who has not come across some incident of bereavement in the family or of close friends? All tragedies and bereavements naturally cause stress but there is a way to cope with them in a creative manner through our positive response. In this chapter, we are giving certain tips which will definitely enable us to cope with different types of tragedies, adverse situations and bereavements in our day-to-day life.

1. Remember, "This will also pass away"

No dark clouds have ever remained in the sky all the time. This is a phenomenon known to all of us. Yet we seem to be oblivious of it when we are faced with a situation causing a great deal of stress to us. A long time ago, there ruled a king who announced that if in the evening bazaar anything displayed by any trader was not sold, he would buy the same at the price asked for. Once a trader reported that he was unable to sell one small packet for which he demanded one lakh rupees. The trader would not disclose the contents of the packet. Hence, nobody was prepared to pay. However, the king according to his promise purchased that small packet, though much against the advice of his minister and paid one lakh rupees to the trader. The king brought the packet to his bedroom and opened it. It was wrapped in paper upon paper and on the last piece of paper was written "This will also pass away". Everybody laughed at the king. However, the king thought that the trader could not have befooled him. Hence, he put that piece of advice in front of his bed in the bedroom. A few days later, there was a rebellion by his nephew and an attack by the neighbouring king. The king got worried. When he looked at this advice, however, he regained calmness, and started preparations to crush the rebellion and to fight the enemy with a calm mind and full preparation. He was successful. Similar moments came again later in his life and everytime, he thought upon the advice: "This will also pass away".

This story has a great moral for us. Whenever we are faced with any momentary stress, we too should keep cool by remembering that "This will also pass away."

2. No body is immortal but every soul is

Most of us are afraid of death. But we must remember that none of us is immortal in this world. Only our soul is immortal.

One thing is certain in this world and that is death. Then why should we be worried about it? If we come across any tragic event, like death of a near and dear relative or of a close friend, etc., we should take it as an act of God, remembering at the same time that the soul is immortal. Lord Krishna in the *Gita* (II.20) says:

"Na jayate mriyate va kadacin
 na'yam bhutva bhavita va na bhuyah
ajo nityah sasvato 'yam purano
 na hanyate hanyamane sarire"

This has been translated by Dr. S. Radhakrishnan as:

"He is never born, nor does he die at any time, nor having (once) come to be will he again cease to be. He is unborn, eternal, permanent and primeval. He is not slain when the body is slain."

Thus, the soul is everlasting, a divine form, and derives its existence from God. Just as people discard old clothes and wear new ones without repenting about the discarded old clothes, so also the soul discards the old body and takes on a new one. Hence, why should we lament over the discarding of the covering of the soul which is the body? If we meditate on this thought, we will be able to cope with tragedies and bereavements in a peaceful manner.

3. Value of tears

On occasions of tragedy and bereavement, tears play an important role to lessen the impact of stress. If tears flow from the eyes of the breaved person, let them flow. In a natural manner, tears help the bereaved person to cope with stress effectively.

4. Let anxiety not cause nervous breakdown

We should remember that in the case of a tragedy or bereavement the core of a nervous breakdown is anxiety. And anxiety is a condition of heightened tension accompanied by an overpowering feeling of apprehension without apparent reason. We should not allow anxiety to cause nervous breakdown. At the time of tragedy and bereavement, the impact of anxiety can be minimised by remembering the inevitability of death, immortality of soul, and temporary nature of the tragedy and bereavement which "will also pass away."

5. Grief has to be wisely handled

One of the greatest moments for grief is death of a relative or of a friend. Such a situation has to be handled very wisely. We should remember that death is also a kind of benevolent act of God because it is only when our fellow creature becomes unfit, has pain instead of pleasure, and becomes an encumberance instead of an aid, that God takes him away. Untimely death is certainly a cause of great grief but even such moments have to be handled with care, through faith in God. If we have to write a condolence letter to the family of a friend we should avoid clichés. We should write about the life of the departed person, his friendliness, fine spirit, gaiety and good qualities and not about his death. We should recall the happy and good moments and particularly, the acts of benevolence of the departed soul. Below is given an illustration of a letter written by Harold J. Laski in 1929 to Justice Oliver Wendell Holmes on the death of Mrs. Holmes:

"You know how big a space you both have filled in our hearts. She had, with all her reserve and reticence, genius for affection. And to see you together was a lesson in the beauty of love. I know that things can never be the same for you again. But I want you to remember that your house was made by her, for me, as for others, a place of loving pilgrimage and that, while we live, she will be remembered with deep affection."

6. Helping a bereaved person with sincere listening

Intelligent listening on our part helps the bereaved person to express what he has in mind and thus helps him ease the stressful effect of the tragedy. People who have a genius for listening always inspire confidence. We should listen to the grief of the grief-stricken and console him or her, as we can. One of the obstacles to good listening is an eagerness to interrupt the speaker. We have to be careful about this, and remember that prayers to God work because God is silent and does not offer advice while listening.

7. Have faith in God

The most effective and potent manner of coping with tragedies and bereavements is to have implicit faith in God. It is said that a person who has faith in God throughout his life is likely to have faith in others, and the most important of all, faith in himself. Faith in ourselves gives us peace and assurance that we will overcome disaster, conflict and bereavement, and reach the goal of our life.

Valmiki's *Ramayana* has also this perennial advice to offer to all of us about equanimity: "Be strong in woe and humble in weal and do not lose your balance in pain or pleasure. Do not befriend anyone too much nor show unfriendliness to any. Both are serious faults; therefore seek the golden mean."

Right Approach Towards *Karma* or Work in Daily Life

***Gita* on selfless work**

The *Gita* (II.47) enunciates Lord Krishna's exposition of *nishkama* (selfless) *karma yoga* through the famous formula for action in day-to-day life as :

*"Karmany evaa 'dhikaaras te
   ma phaleshu kadaacana
ma karma phala hetur bhur
   ma te sango'stv akarmani."*

Thus we should be concerned with the performance, the act, and not with its result or returns. "Let not the results motivate thy actions therefore, but do not (for that reason) fall into 'inaction' either." This is what the *Gita* has proclaimed. An outstanding feature of this philosophy is that though the 'spirit' is actionless, bodily activity is necessary for attaining spiritual perfection. So the sensible thing to do is to give up the idea of 'doership' and let the body and mind act according to their urges in which they are by duty prone or by habit accustomed. We should continue to live in the world discharging our duties outwardly, our mind remaining anchored in the inward quiet of our spirithood (*Gita* V, 8-9). The merit of an action lies not so much in its outer nature or results as in its contribution towards one's spiritual growth. According to this *Karma yoga* of the *Gita*, work is its own reward.

Attitude towards *Prarabdha*

The true philosophy of *Karma yoga* makes it necessary for us to understand the true significance of *prarabdha*, because many a time despite hard work results do not come up to our expectation. This is mainly because of the play of *prarabdha*. Very often a question is asked: suppose a devotee has unflinching faith in God; does it in anyway help him to get rid of his *prarabdha*?

It is necessary for us to understand the theory of *prarabdha*. From our previous births, we carried forward impressions, both good and bad, which have set in motion our present life. It is everybody's knowledge that a person's worldly business account ends in a net gain or a net loss. This karmic account retains both good and bad entries. Everyone has to suffer because of his or her past demerits or enjoy because of his or her merits. What we are today is the effect of our past *karma*. So the question of the future is open to us. It will be shaped by our present. Between the future and the past there is continuous change which takes place in the present. He who lives in the past is dead even as he who lives in the future is never born. Hence, a serious reckoning of the present (the *prarabdha* i.e. the fructifying *karma*), is the sign of sanity. Our Indian scriptures say "*avashyameva bhoktavyam kritam karma shubhashubham*", i.e., one has to reap the fruits of one's actions, both virtuous and sinful. The fructifying *karmas* are exhausted only by reaping the results, and when all the *prarabdhas* are destroyed, the manifested universe vanishes. Only through selfless *karma* or work can we end the effect of *prarabdha*. If we choose to end *prarabdha* and accordingly make a move in the right direction through surrender to God and selfless work without expectation of reward, only then does the question of God's intervention arise. True understanding of *prarabdha* is absolutely essential for right living.

Our approach towards *karma* today
What is essential for very good living, particularly in a spiritual way, is an effort to do our duty with equanimity of mind and without bothering ourselves with the positive or negative effects of *karma*. We should only remember that today's *karma* will not only determine the result today but will also form the future *prarabdha*, the shaping of which is absolutely in our hands. The best way of tackling or settling worry is through a right approach towards work at present.

Similar sentiments were expressed by Thomas Carlyle, who

in *Past and Present*, said, "Blessed is he who has found his work; let him ask no other blessedness. He has a work, a life-purpose; he has found it and will follow it." Even worldly achievements and successes are the result of work and work only, as Thomas Alva Edison rightly said, "I never did anything worth doing by accident; nor did any of my inventions come by accident; they came by work." The necessity for work will always remain. That is why Henry Ford has gone to the extent of saying, "There will never be a system invented which will do away with the necessity for work."

Purity of Mind, Heart and Action in Daily Life

Control of mind is necessary for purity

For purity of life, it is essential that we have proper control of mind which implies control of impure or evil thoughts. A question is generally asked: 'Why do evil thoughts arise in the mind?' The very fact that we experience mental suffering due to evil thoughts is a sign of spiritual progress. This is because many persons do not have even that much of sensitivity. For some people it is very difficult to keep the mind pure and unruffled, because of their deep-rooted worldly *samskaras*, unfavourable surroundings and several other extrovert tendencies. To others, evil thoughts are not a problem at all. They appear occasionally as a passing phase without doing much havoc. Hence, we have to watch our mind very carefully. We have to be constantly vigilant and be on the alert. We should not allow the waves of irritability, jealousy, anger, hatred and lust disturb us. The best remedy for this is to meditate on the attributes of the Lord, or to draw our attention to a new interesting realm. We may divert our attention by studying the lives of great saints. Lord Krishna in the *Gita* (XVI.1) talks about some of the important qualities of a god-like person:

"Abhayam sattvasamsuddhir
  jnanayogavyavasthitih
danam damas ca yajnas ca
  suvadhyayas tapa arjavam"

This has been translated by Dr. S. Radhakrishnan as under:

"The blessed Lord said that a good man possesses the qualities of fearlessness, purity of mind, wise apportionment of knowledge and concentration, charity, self-control and sacrifice, study of the scriptures, austerity and uprightness".

Certain further qualities of non-violence, truth, freedom from anger, forgiveness, etc. are described in two further verses of the *Gita*. For a day-to-day spiritual living, it is absolutely essential to have these qualities which will ensure purity of mind and heart.

Faith in oneself is absolutely essential

For our journey towards attaining purity of mind and heart it is absolutely essential to have faith in our own selves. We must remember that we are our own friend and our own enemy. This has been beautifully expressed by Lord Krishna in the *Gita* (VI.5):

"Uddhared atmanatmanam
  na 'tmanam avasadayet
atmai'va hy atmano bandhur
  atmai'va ripur atmanah"

This has been translated by Dr. S. Radhakrishnan as:

"Let a man lift himself by himself, let him not degrade himself; for the self alone is the friend of the self and the self alone is the enemy of the self."

We have to remember that the supreme self is within us. It is the consciousness of everyday life. But we are unaware of the self in us because our attention is engaged by objects which we like or dislike. If we do not realise the pointlessness, the irrelevance and the squalour of our ordinary life, the true self becomes the enemy of our ordinary life. The universal self and the personal self are not antagonistic to each other. The universal self can be a friend or a foe of the personal self. If our impulses are under control, and if our personal self offers itself to the universal self, then the latter becomes our guide. In order to succeed in controlling the mind we must have in addition to a strong will, faith in ourselves and follow the advice of Lord Krishna as mentioned above. For this, we have to have moral principles and regularity in life. We must check the proverbial restlessness of the mind. We must avoid assiduously the impurities of mind like envy, hatred, anger, fear, jealousy, lust, greed, temptation, etc.

Satsang helps in attaining purity of mind and heart

One of the sure ways of controlling mind and attaining purity of mind, heart and action is to seek the company of perfect or fully realised sages or souls. The powerful aura of their holiness will penetrate us and bring about a speedy change in our mind. As long as we have desires other than that of realising God, it will be difficult to control the mind. It is holy company which roots out all attachments that are impediments in controlling the mind. We must, therefore, remember that one of the excellent ways in which we can usefully spend our time to derive immense spiritual joy and happiness is to look for spiritual fellowship or to attend a discourse by some learned religious preacher or saint. We become spiritually living when we are grafted in *satsang*. Fortunately, in almost all the towns and cities of India, *satsangs* or religious discourses are held periodically, where great saints and religious preachers like Morari Bapu, Shri Asha Ram Bapu, Bhaiji, Sudhanshu Ji Maharaj, Ma Amritanandmayi and saints and sages of Shri Ramkrishna Mission, Swami Chinmaya Mission and Aurobindo Mission give discourses not only in English and Hindi, but also in various regional languages. We should take part in such *satsangs* and derive immense happiness and spiritual joy. We can complement this by a visit to holy places and pilgrimage centres.

Meditation on God

One of the most fashionable terms throughout the world today is 'meditation'. But one who does not know how to meditate and simply tries to force meditation as a fashion, may find it very difficult to do so. It cannot be gainsaid that our true nature is happiness. We want to discover everlasting happiness. Disappointed with the outside world, we time and again turn inward to seek this elusive happiness and peace. It is this turning within, this search for the truth of one's being, which is termed as the practice of meditation. Meditation is the effortless abiding faith in the awareness of one's true nature. For a *jnani*, i.e., a self-realised person, meditation is the natural state. Having realised the nature of self, one is in a state of pure consciousness. This is an advanced stage and can be reached only after making some spiritual progress. However, most of us fall in the category of a seeker. A seeker has to practise constantly and diligently to be aware of the self. As a first step towards this establishment in the self, the attention of the mind is turned away from the sense objects towards the self. Swami Muktananda of Ganeshpuri has laid great emphasis on the worship of the self. He has introduced a new type of meditation based on the awakening of *kundalani shakti* through *Siddha yoga*. Under this system, through the grace of an enlightened guru or a *siddha*, one automatically goes into the state of meditation. The meditator has to realise his self through the thought: "I am pure consciousness" or "*Aham Brahamasmi*", i.e., "I am the Brahama or Supreme Self". In the *Bhagvad Gita* (VI.18), Lord Krishna says, "When the perfectly controlled mind, free from longing for the object of the world is turned towards the self, it abides in the self." And this is meditation.

It is always better to learn meditation from a guru. The chief advantage of meditation is contentment and peace. Thus, we get what is known as infinite happiness.

Peace of mind through purity
Everybody wants peace. As Pope John Paul II said, "If we wish to have true peace, we must give it a soul. The soul of peace is love. It is love that gives life to peace, more than victory or defeat, more than self-interest or fear or weariness or need.

The soul of peace is love, which for us believers comes from the love of God and exercises itself in love for men."

About purity and peace, St. Vincent de Paul has beautifully said, "A very powerful and efficacious medicament, and the means to purify ourselves from every imperfection, to overcome all temptations and to preserve in our heart imperturbable peace, is conformity to the will of God."

And this is possible in day-to-day living.

Positive Attitude to Avoid Stress and Tension

Maintain an equipoise with a balanced mind

It is a common experience of all human beings that happiness and sorrow alternate in our day-to-day life. Likewise, difficulties and obstacles are faced by most of us, many a time during our life. These can affect the mind and compromise the sense of duty. And when this happens, we make many mistakes. The result is that we are reborn to mitigate the effects of wrong actions and we deviate from the path of *nirvana*, i.e. freedom from the cycle of births and deaths. Hence, it is absolutely imperative for us not to allow happiness or sorrow to affect our minds. Rather, we should try to maintain an equipoise with a balanced mind and proper discrimination. One of the greatest tools for coping with stress is the principle of equanimity as enunciated again and again by Lord Krishna in the *Bhagavad Gita* where He talks of "equanimity" in the wonderful phrase *"samatvam yoga ucchayate"*, i.e., "*yoga* is equanimity".

Our correct attitude in life should be not to feel too much elated at things which are said to be favourable to us. Likewise, we should not get depressed or put ourselves under stress or feel grieved when things are against our liking or we are unnecessarily criticised. Thus, we should have equipoise or equanimity both in moments of joy and despair, gain and loss, appreciation and criticism. This principle, if practised well, will certainly enable us to cope with stress and tension effectively and enable us to lead a happy and purposeful life.

Every problem has a solution

We often come across situations which cause us stress. And stress is a response to demand. Hence, a positive reponse to the various demands made on us helps in coping with stress and enables us to have a purposeful living. It is we who should choose to behave the way we do. It is not the world around us which makes us do what we do. For example, our getting angry or remaining calm is our own conscious or unconscious decision. Hence, if we believe with sincerity that every problem has a solution, we will be able to tackle the stress related problems easily. We should not be afraid of problems in life. Rather, we should derive inspiration from the spirit of Charles F. Kettering of General Motors who said that problems are the price of progress. He used to say, "Don't bring me anything but trouble. Good news weakens me." We can derive inspiration from the British physicist and Cambrige University Mathematics professor Stephen Hawking, who has persevered through the pain and distress of a rare degenerative muscle disease to become the world's foremost mathematician, occupying the chair of Sir Issac Newton. There are many striking examples of positive responses to situations causing stress and tension, which reveal patience, resilience and forgiveness. We can learn from these examples.

Four types of response

The great Rishi Patanjali in *Yogasutras* (I.33) has suggested the proper attitudes to be held towards four types of people. These are :
(1) friendliness towards the happy,
(2) compassion for the unhappy,
(3) delight in the virtuous, and
(4) indifference towards the wicked.

If we meet someone who is happy in his way of life, we are inclined to envy him and be jealous of his success. But Patanjali says that we must learn to rejoice in it; we must be pleased in it just as we take pleasure in the happiness of a friend.

If someone is unhappy, we should feel sorry for him, instead of despising him or criticising him for bringing misfortunes upon himself.

Again, the virtues of others is apt to irritate us. But Patanjali suggests that we should delight in it and see it as an inspiration for ourselves to do better.

As regards the fourth type of people, namely, the wicked, our normal response is hatred and injury. We may succeed in injuring a wicked person, but we should remember that we shall be injuring ourselves much more, and our hatred will throw our own minds into confusion. Hence, Patanjali suggests that we should practise indifference when we feel hurt.

Emotions, attitudes and feelings can be explosive

We should remember that if emotions, attitudes and feelings are not properly controlled, they can prove to be explosive and the explosion could be violent. It would be visible to any observer when we lose control of ourselves in a fit of rage or anger. However, the violence can also be only inside us while outwardly we may appear to be quite calm and full of poise. But either way, violence is harmful. Emotion is considered good if it relaxes us and prevents us from growing tense.

Hope is an important aspect in the prevention of tension. Supposing the statistical statement about a particular disease says: "Only five per cent of the people with your disease has survived." In that case, remember: "Those who survive, survive hundred per cent". It is on the foundation of such optimism that the tense situation can be mastered.

Say 'no' to anger

When we lose control of ourselves in a fit of anger we have an explosive situation. It is absolutely essential for excellent living that we should say 'no' to anger. We should remember the wise words of Glendale: "Anger is an acid that can do more harm to the vessel in which it is stored than to anything on which it is poured." Hence, we must learn to tackle the situation causing anger and remain either absolutely silent or divert our attention from the situation to something else.

We might recall an actual incident which occured during the course of the American Civil War in 1860-61, when a Major General of the Army disobeyed the orders of the Secretary of War, Edwin Stanton. Stanton went to the US President, Abraham Lincoln. He said, "I would like to give a piece of my mind to that man. Please advise me on what to do". Lincoln replied, "You write to him what you have on your mind. You make it as sharp as possible; cut him up". Thereupon, Stanton showed the nasty letter which he wrote to that officer, to the President. The President appreciated the letter. Thereupon, Stanton said, "When can I send it? Can I send it now to the Major General?" Lincoln's reply was classic: "What? Send it? Why send it at all? why, why, why... Don't send it at all, tear it up. It is better if you put it in the stove. Now you have freed your mind on the subject; that was necessary; you never want to send such a letter; I would never do so."

Forgiveness

One of the best ways of avoiding tension and negative thoughts is to remember the great virtue of forgiveness and to implement it in actual practice. It is rightly said by George Herbert, "He who cannot forgive others, destroys the bridge over which he himself must pass." If we cultivate the habit of forgiving others we tend to forget the wrong done to us and thus, we do not keep the wound open. The wounds heal themselves very fast once we indulge in forgiveness. In this connection, it would be wise to remember what

Confucius said: "To be wronged is nothing, unless we continue to remember it." Lord Mahavir also hailed the great quality of forgiveness.

Another aspect of forgiveness is that if we do any harm to others, we should be gracious enough to ask for forgiveness.

Non-attachment

The virtue of non-attachment is an important element of positive attitude and has been rightly stressed by the great sages and saints of the world. Patanjali, in *Yogasutras* (I.15), says that non-attachment is self-mastery; it is freedom from desire for what is seen or heard. In fact, non-attachment is the exercise of discrimination. We gradually gain control of the impure thought waves by asking ourselves, "Why do I really desire that object? What permanent advantage should I gain by possessing it? In what manner would its possession help me towards knowledge and freedom?" The answers to these questions are always disconcerting. They would normally show us that the desired object is not only useless as a means to liberation but potentially harmful as a means to ignorance and bondage.

Learn from failure

During the course of our life, we are bound to have certain experiences which are not very enjoyable. These may be due to our failures in our life. But there is no cause of keeping our spirits down. We should rather remember that adversity is the state in which a human being more easily becomes acquainted with himself. Success is a definite state of mind but affirmative; failure is also a definite state of mind, but negative. So we should refrain from gloating over our past failures. Rather, we should learn to achieve success in future. The famous novelist Melville gave a sound piece of advice to people who fail in life: "He who has never failed somewhere, that man cannot be great." We should remember that life is a succession of failures but fortunately, most of them are little ones.

Selfless Service to All Creatures

Service to others is the hall-mark of spirituality

In this concluding chapter, we shall be discussing the virtue of selfless service in day-to-day living. It is said that if the highest expression of spirituality is seeing God dwelling in the hearts of all, then true worship is offering service to mankind. Sri Ramakrishna consistently stressed serving human beings as God himself — worshipping *Jiva* as Shiva.

His life reflected his belief. Swami Vivekananda expanded on this theme, both in words and actions. He said (CW.3 : 142): "He who sees Shiva in the poor, in the weak, and in the diseased, really worships Shiva, and if he sees Shiva only in the image, his worship is but preliminary."

We would also do well to meditate on the thought given by Epictetus: "One cannot pursue one's own highest good without at the same time necessarily promoting the good of others. A life based on narrow self-interest cannot be esteemed by any honourable measurement. Seeking the very best in ourselves means actively caring for the welfare of other human beings."

Get involved in service activities

A human being is not only concerned with his own personal welfare but also with the welfare of his group. We feel joy when we give because basically, we are satisfying an inmate desire.

For doing service to other human beings and fellow creatures, we need not have a lot of money. Even with little or no money, we can do a lot of service. For example, one of the best ways to get involved in social service is to visit a local hospital and talk to the patients lovingly. We may also consider joining service clubs like Lions' or Rotary Club or Red Cross. We should also try to assume civic reponsibilities. We should show genuine compassion when we come across a person who deserves sympathetic attention. If we participate in the experiences of others, our own experience is amplified and we achieve higher understanding and spiritual progress.

Recipe for service in daily life

I have composed a short poem which is a sort of recipe for selfless service:

"O, Ladies and Gentlemen!
Please take a sizeable quantity of cheerfulness in a large bucket.
And let it simmer without stopping
Add a heaped tablespoon full of thoughtfulness towards the fellow beings.
Sprinkle the essence of charity and sympathy to all.
Stir them well together
Strain off all particles of selfishness and prejudices from it

Finally when the dish is ready
Please serve it with the sauce of love towards all,
and malice towards none."

An inspiring anecdote of service

We all remember several acts of service done by others. I remember a very unselfish, ethical act of true service displayed by the owner of a small wayside vegetarian hotel. On October 8, 2000, me and my wife, Asha Rani Lakhotia, left New Delhi by car to attend the funeral of an old relative in Sahaswan town of Badayun District of U.P. We reached Hapur city at about 1.00 p.m. and decided to stop for lunch. We noticed a small vegetarian hotel at the road crossing. The owner of the hotel was one Mr. Agarwal. When we enquired about the rates, Mr. Agarwal said, "We charge Rs. 15 per *thali*, in which besides *chapatis* and rice, there will be two vegetables, *dahi-raita* and pickles." We ordered three *thalis* – two for us and one for the driver. We also took one extra plate of curd priced at Rs.5. When we finished our lunch, I handed over a fifty-rupee note to the hotel owner, that being the cost of the three *thalis* and the curd. But Mr. Agarwal, the owner, returned Rs. 15 to me saying that he would be charging Rs. 5 less per *thali*. I was surprised and enquired about the reason. Thereupon, Mr. Agarwal said, "Sir, you have not eaten the full *thali*. People eat even more than eight *chapatis* and rice per *thali* and still we charge only Rs. 15. As you have eaten much less, we will charge Rs. 10. I have to give an account of myself to God, you know."

We were highly surprised to hear these words from a simple owner of a small wayside hotel: he displayed such great ethical values. This was a very unique and pleasant experience for us and this simple gentleman has left an indelible impression upon my mind.

Other titles in the series

- Kundalini
- Kriya Yoga
- Reiki
- Astrology
- Hypnosis
- Mantras
- Meditation
- Vastushastra
- Aromatherapy
- Psychic Development
- Yoga for Health and Happiness